Cat Hepburn is an award winning scr
artist based between Glasgow and Be
nationally and internationally across s
the likes of BBC6 Music Festival, Edinl
4. She is the author of the poetry book ... ɔɪʀʟɪ ١○○ᗪ, which she
developed into a hit solo spoken word theatre show in 2019.
Cat is also the co-founder of Sonnet Youth, one of Scotland's
leading spoken word nights.

*"As engaging on page as she is on stage, Hepburn consistently
outdoes herself with courage, grace and humour."*
Darren 'Loki' McGarvey

Dating
&
Other Hobbies

Cat Hepburn

Burning Eye

Burning Eye Books
Never Knowingly
Mainstream

This edition published by Burning Eye Books 2021

www.burningeye.co.uk

@burningeyebooks

Burning Eye Books
15 West Hill, Portishead, BS20 6LG

ISBN 978-1-913958-04-6

Dating
&
Other Hobbies

To Marie Claire, for all the good times at DDHQ;
the ones we can remember… and the ones we can't.

CONTENTS

MISTAKES OF A TWENTY-SOMETHING MILLENNIAL

Ordering that second bottle of wine
on a school night.
Losing track of time.
Sleeping with him.
Sleeping with her.
Not going to sleep.
Sleeping in.
Sleeping on a couch at a party.
Going to sleep with
your makeup on,
or your bra.
Making him sleep on the couch
when you know deep down that
you are in the wrong.
Wearing a thong.
Not following a recipe.
Choosing
the wrong karaoke song,
the wrong university course,
the wrong main course,
the wrong contraception,
the wrong person to
give your affection.
Wearing high heels
that you can't walk in
to a winter wedding reception
in Scotland.
Getting the bus
instead of walking
in the fresh air.
Cutting your own hair.

Not telling someone exactly
how you feel.

Telling someone exactly
how you feel.

Stealing cheese from Tesco.
Thinking it's not an interview.
Worrying about your pubes.
Berating your own boobs.
Being too afraid to get
your bare legs out.
Telling a secret,
even if it was yours to let out.
Letting out someone else's pet.
Smoking cigarettes.
Taking too much ketamine,
or any amphetamine.
Not wearing SPF.
Kissing a colleague,
or worse,
someone else's boyfriend.
Missing a person who made you feel
terrible.
Drawing on eyebrows/cheekbones terribly.

Getting your dinner delivered
instead of working out.
Abusing your liver.
Not taking a jacket on a night out.
Ghosting somebody who didn't deserve it.
Spreading yourself too thin.
Squeezing yourself into skinny jeans.
Wishing you were thinner,
or hotter.
Not drinking enough water.
Worrying about what people think.
Not taking vitamin D.
Getting an embarrassing tattoo.
Holding in a poo at a boy's flat.
Forgetting to brush your teeth.

Answering an inappropriate person's DMs.
Sliding into an inappropriate person's DMs.

But are these all mistakes,
or ways we find to grow and learn,
earn our stripes
and discover who we are?
When we're old in rocking chairs,
what else are we going to sit
and think about for fun –
but all the questionable decisions
that we made when we were young?

chapter 1

digital

WHAT'S YOUR TYPE?

CrossFit fanatics
with designer dicks.

Girls with short fringes
who are into politics.

Bespectacled cardigan-wearing
Guardian readers.

Broad-shouldered rugby buffs
who spray in their receders.

Pasty eco-warriors
who look like they don't wash.

Tall toothy horsey people
who don't like being called posh.

Wiry academics who smoke rollies
and drink craft beer.

Coke-snorting DJs
who have problems being sincere.

Curvaceous lassies
bearing tattooed angel wings.

Dominant older women
who love to use sex swings.

Men with big wallets,
shiny heads and shiny shoes.

Spice boys who get their teeth whitened
and like to shop in Cruise.

Guitar-playing beach bums
too stoned to call you back.

Angular-jawed handsome
megalomaniacs.

Steroid-taking fuckboys
who only wear North Face.

Busty garden fanatics
who have expensive taste.

Shorter-than-average life-and-souls
always telling jokes.

Emotionally unavailable
artistic commitment-phobes.

Skater chicks with piercings,
tats,
fake tan and Vans.

Gobby daddy's girls
who talk loudly
with their hands.

Overly assertive cat people
with a penchant for merlot.

Bearded men who drink tequila
and practise stick-and-poke.

Extrovert socialists
who tweet more than they march.

Workies with great chat who
look sexy driving cars.

Smoothie-drinking gym bunnies
with peachy bubble bums.

Men who look like bikers
but still live with their mums.

False-nail-wearing
sarcastic single mothers.

Kind-hearted
introverted
wannabe drummers.

Shaved-headed punks
who bake their own bread.

People who, the minute you're over,
will sleep with your best friend.

CRUSH

Her Nice'n Easy
brassy, yet
somehow
classy mane
flows almost
down to her bum,
straightened to within
an inch of its life
with an iron
borrowed from her mum.
The smell of Impulse 'Why Not?'
and burning hair on brown paper
surrounds her in a potent haze.

She stays up late,
smokes B&H ciggies
out her window,
and when her mum
and stepdad go away
she has the sickest empties.
An open-minded
and sparky
only child,
she's allowed
to go pretty wild.
She has two pet mice;
she named them Britney and Christina.
Her belly button is pierced twice.
Every fourth-year girl
is desperate to be her.

His family is
comparatively
rudderless,
sadly motherless;
his house was built

with bricks of
testosterone
and denial.

His brothers spend
most of their time
pumping iron
and bragging about
pumping birds.
They are pure tough
guys,
a wee bit of rough
guys,
number 1
buzz cut,
knuckles cut up
from scrapping
at the weekends
guys.

He's not like them;
he's softer,
sweeter,
a decent boy
with his head screwed on.
He doesn't get satisfaction
from headbutting
a random to
        shut him up!
He thinks
girls are special,
not
        skanky little sluts.

She
paints on her confidence
with lip-gloss ease;
the V
of her thong
sprouts from the back

of her tight black
scousers
like blooming lilacs
in summer.

But, best of all,
she's not daft.
She answers questions
in class
with intelligence
and sass.

The very knowledge
of her presence makes
his blood pump faster
to places that he really
wished it wouldn't.
It cuts through
paper aeroplanes
and laughter.
Sharing a maths
classroom
with her is
pain and pleasure
in equal measures.

He does not
talk
about his feelings;
he's learnt from the best
to internalise them.
He has
anxiety,
but there's not a
word for it yet;
that will come way later,
in his thirties,
when he goes to therapy
every second Tuesday

like the rest of his arty
middle-class pals.

She's the one
who asks him out
and he's shocked;
he can't believe his luck.
The prettiest girl in school
wants to hook up.

And in a few weeks
they go from messaging
every day
to kissing to
second base,
then S-E-X,
high on young love
and exploration,
every chance they get:
in her bottom bunk bed,
next to the flower beds
by Aldi,
back row of the cinema
watching that new film
Alfie.
He doesn't wear a johnny
'cause his brother Jonjo
says
it's like

> *showering wi' a raincoat on.*
> *Dinnae bother, mate;*
> *it's bareback or nothin' at aw.*

Then two
little blue
lines
come along
and spoil
all the fun.

She's fifteen
and has dreams
of going traveling
and then to uni,
so there's no question
about what to do.
The word abortion
is on the tip
of both of their tongues.
She's not ready
to be a mum.

After the procedure,
he can't find his words;
they appear to have
run away from home
with his feelings in tow.
All he needs to do is tell her
        it's all gonna be OK
but he stays
mute
not knowing what to say.

It hurts
and she's sensible
enough
to know
that it was
the right thing,
whatever that means,
but the real sting
comes from his silence;
it screams out to her
like a void.
She feels
almost destroyed
by that boy.

His big-mouthed
wee brother
finds out,
which means
so does everyone
at school;
she takes a few weeks off
to avoid the relentless
rumour mill.

Now he sees
what she's up to
from the odd
social media post;
he muted her years ago
but he still clicks
on them
from time to time.
Her hair
is now a graduated bob
and light brown
but she has
that same cheeky smile.

One day he sees a photo
of her on Instagram;
she's beaming,
holding a picture
of her twelve-week scan.
By her side
is the soon-to-be-dad,
a tall,
sandy-coloured man
with a beard
and a beanie hat.

It makes him realise
that he hadn't
treated her

in the way
that she deserved;
they were trying on
adulthood
like ill-fitting
baggy suits
that didn't suit them,
adolescents
with no direction
and too much affection
and hormones
and he was a prick.

Would
or could
she ever
forgive him?

He badly wants to
reach out to her,
to tell her that now
he is all grown up,
he has found his words,
and that his brothers
were a bunch of dafties,
and that he hopes
that she's happy
and knows that she
was his true first love
and he thinks about her lots.

His thumbs are poised
like stalemate snakes
to write all of this out
in a DM
but he
just gives the photo
a like instead.

CIRCLE OF SHAME

The sidebar of 'harmless fluff'
in the Daily Fail
teaches us
to hate ourselves
and other women
and men,
but, hey,
if they tell us
what new lipstick to buy
it makes it OK, then.

They repeat the same old
rhetoric about
our potential beauty
and good health,
claiming to reveal
that elusive secret
that will finally
make us happy;
our problems will vanish
if we exude wealth.

On the glossy surface
and a glance at their interior
they look fun,
but they're designed
to make us feel inferior.

Size-zero models on every page
encouraging the newest diet fad;
they are there to make clothes
look good
and us feel bad.

Obsessive and obscene
celebrity culture,

paps circling round people
like hungry vultures,
waiting to get the money shot
of them getting out a taxi cab,
camera right under the skirt,
hoping to snap
the complete lack
of pants.

Mindless gossip
fabricated
and exaggerated rumours
growing in young minds
like deadly tumours.
Spending time
on our appearance
is not a want but a need;
the illusion
of personal choice
is beginning to recede.

Look how this
multi-millionairess
has managed to lose
all her baby weight
and squeeze her arse
into a tight dress.

Shame on all you
normal women
without personal trainers
and home gyms.
Your life would be fine
if only you were thin.

Adverts on every single page
encouraging you to
spend
spend
spend,

spend money
that you don't have,
take out a loan,
increase your overdraft,
get a credit card,
get into debt
to get that great handbag;
it's a must-have.

They promote
slut shaming,
nasty naming,
demonisation,
fame turning on
and attacking
its very own
creations.

The magnification
of flaws,
mistakes,
problems
and normality;
these sites are a threat
to our society.

Star goes makeup-free
as she steps out her house;
you can see her
un-matching bra
through that blouse;
crow's feet,
bingo wings,
saggy tum,
cellulite bum,
ooft,
she's piled on
the pounds
after being dumped.

A woman who is famous
for her ability to sing
vilified for leaving her house
without her wedding ring.

The circle of shame;
can you believe that she's
worn that outfit again?

Tips and tricks to change
yourself
so he will love you more.

A quiz:
how much sex are you having?
Are you a virgin or a whore?
Nine telltale signs
that your boyfriend
is cheating on you.
All your problems
will be solved when
you buy this killer shoe.

A new magical cream
to make your skin
look flawless,
rewind and reverse
the natural ageing process.

Now I'm old enough
to make my own decisions
and look at things
objectively
and critically,
but it's not me
that I'm worried
about.

It's the young
and impressionable,
little girls and boys
who are taught from
a young age to play
with certain toys,
to act a certain way
towards one another,
be strong and dominant
like a father
or weak and soft
like a mother.

Compare their imperfections
to Photoshopped creations,
an alternative reality of
unrealistic expectations.

Misogyny is at its most toxic
when it's turned
inwards,
encouraging us to spend money
we don't have,
raising a generation of girls
who care more about the thigh gap
than the pay gap.

FOR THE GRAM

I prefer Instalife
'cause real life's
shite.
Real life is bad hair days,
period pain and acne,
low self-esteem,
depression and anxiety.

Online life
is shiny and new,
dewy skin
and the power of youth,
freckles and hearts
and flower crowns,
booty workouts,
shopping labels
in town,
emojis used
in every interaction,
reels provide me
with an addictive
distraction.

Get those filters on
so I don't look human,
not a pore in sight
even when
you zoom in.
My existence
is displayed
in small bitesize
squares,
white teeth,
perfect hair.
Fine lines:
they're not there!

Airbrushed,
polished,
my problems erased,
getting adoration
for my Outfit of the Day;
a direct hit of dopamine
goes to my bloodstream
for every digital heart
that beats my way.

Are they hot dogs or legs?
I want people to say
when I put up the pics
from my recent holiday
where everything
that I planned
was actually
for the gram.

Let me hold your baby
or dog on my lap
so I can get a snap
for that new dating app.
I'll post Boomerangs
of champagne clinking,
TikToks of me dancing,
and use hashtags to convey
exactly what I'm thinking.

I want to show
that I'm
sexy,
smart
and sweet
from a cheeky fleet
that I put up of my feet.

Strike a pose,
zero fucks given,
squad goals,
healthy living.
Give me all the followers
and likes
to keep me warm at night.
There's safety in hiding
behind a screen.
Real life hurts;
fuck showing
the real me.

SELFIE

You were trying to be nice,
you took the photo thrice,
but when you walked away
I deleted them,
then took a selfie.

FAKE BAKE KNEES

Two besties sit
sipping
espresso martinis
in an aspirational bar
with polished surfaces
and polished people.
The tables are full of
men with taught pecs
wearing tight jeans
and glaring white trainers
and women with
highlighter-
bright
faces.
The smell of Creed
chats up
the smell of Miss Dior
in the air.

The girls both have
eye-lash strips
cat eye flicks,
manicured tips,
pouting lips,
and one has rips
in her skinny jeans
meaning
segments
of orange
beam
from her
fake bake knees.

Her nails claw
at her iPhone;
the glow

bottom-lights
her diamond-cut jaw
as she talks.
She looks
almost ghoulish,
her face haunted
by all the bad dates
and ghosting and
disappointing
foolish hook-ups.
The dates that
lied about their height,
or weight,
or made her wait,
or didn't show up at all,
all scrawled in
invisible ink
on her dermal filler cheeks.

Oblivious to the group
of peacocking men
trying to catch her
attention
behind her,
she leans on the bar
and she scrolls
through twenty-six photos
of her in her bra.

> *Which one should I send?*
> *This one or that?*
> *I like my arm in this one,*
> *but my face looks all fat.*

> *You look fit in that other one,*
her best mate replies,
and together,
with military precision,
they pick a filter,
then send it to a guy.

TOOTHBRUSH

I don't do relationships. I live by the rule of never letting any guy, or girl, hang around longer than a toothbrush. And, with a very strict personal hygiene routine, I know to replace my toothbrush every three to four months – or when the bristles look tired.

I'm a wedding singer, and on this Friday in spring I've been hired to perform at the wedding of Robert and Stephanie, who met at the legendary nightclub Brix in the city centre back in their raving days. I arrive at the basic bitch three-star hotel and head straight for the toilets. Making my way across the outskirts of the function room that is in desperate need of a new carpet, I notice that the happy couple have named the tables after nineties dance tunes. I say *couple*, but we all know it was Stephanie's idea. Weddings aren't for the groom; marriage is.

Whilst the speeches drag on predictably longer than they were scheduled for, I apply my postbox-red lipstick in the cracked mirror. I can hear a couple shagging in the cubicle nearest to the window. Weddings don't make me especially horny, but they seem to do something to other people. The scuffles and grunting tell me that the loo couple are as keen to keep quiet as they are incapable. I blot my lips on a tissue carefully.

'Don't peak too soon!' I call out to them as I leave.

A skinny young woman in an ill-fitting strapless dress asks a guy with a shaved head where the fuck 'Louis' is. All I can do is hope that's him in the toilets with a random girl he met over the hors d'oeuvres at the champagne reception.

I've seen it all before in this job: the groom snogging his best man, the mother of the bride fainting headfirst into the wedding cake, and, most disturbingly, a human shite in the middle of a labyrinth. Oh the glamour.

I take a discreet seat by the bar and flick my white-blonde Hollywood wave hair, knowing that my off-shoulder, figure-hugging velvet dress is probably catching the attention of a few half-cut husbands' wandering eyes. Not my problem I'm hot. I sip on water and fresh lemon and wait patiently for the best man to wrap up his frighteningly uncomedic monologue. His face is crimson with the overconsumption of pale ale; even the groom's beginning to look fed up.

The sound tech, a guy in his fifties with a frazzled ginger ponytail, signals to me when it's my time to take to the stage. I take a deep breath and step into the lights.

The couple's first dance song is a rendition of a tune I used to listen to when I was drinking cider in parks as a teenager. Neither natural dancers, Stephanie and Robert hold on to each other, swaying awkwardly, everyone's eyes on them. It baffles me how so many people put themselves through traditions that are so clearly uncomfortable for them.

Stephanie's squad, the trussed-up Glesga birds, are the first to take to the dance floor after that. They blink under thick strips of false eyelashes like hand-me-down dollies, and wobble on shiny nude high heels. I admire these women. They can't walk for shit, but that doesn't stop them shoving their feet into those shoes for every special occasion from christenings to an end-of-season River Island sale. Their husbands and boyfriends dutifully bring them large white wines or gin and slims, and they shake their bums to my singing whilst swirling their straws with stiletto-shaped manicured nails.

The 'other halves' of the women are mostly tanned and gurning gym types sporting three-piece suits, their shirts rolled up to reveal sleeve tattoos of religious iconography, angels, clouds and the like. The majority of them have immaculate skin fades and white powder rings circling their nostrils. This type of man exclusively buys in rounds, ensuring every single one of his mates has a drink in their hand. My wee sister Anna likes them: Spice Boys. They're laddy and loud, but they lap up my renditions of diva ballads like thirsty dogs. They sing along to the words, put their ties around their heads and shout requests at me in between numbers. An audience is an audience is an audience.

After an hour and a half of songs that everyone from your ten-year-old to your granny would know the words to, I passionately belt out the last few lines of my finisher. A leathery older woman sings along with me, not even coming close to hitting the same notes. I extend a hand down to her and huskily thank the audience into the mic.

'A special shout out to the bride and groom, Stephanie and Robert; congratulations, you two!'

I spot Robert at the bar doing a shot of something bright blue, the back of his hand flying to his mouth as he almost heaves it up. Stephanie crouches down, posing for a snap with her two little flower girls, one on each arm. Enjoy it, babe. It's probably all downhill from here.

The break in entertainment causes the dance floor to disperse to the bar and the bogs, allowing the DJ, a sweaty man in a backwards baseball cap, shirt and chinos who is waiting in the wings, to set up his CDJs.

A polite smile plastered on my face, I walk through the toxic grey fog of cackling cigarette smokers outside the hotel's entrance. I climb into my baby-pink Fiat 500, take my heels off, slip my feet gratefully into some comfy trainers and check my phone.

There's a notification from a threesome app I've been using for about a year. I've found this particular app to be the most efficient for this type of hook-up.

Threesomes are slightly more effort, but the rewards are more than worth it, in my experience. I enjoy being the sexy fresh addition to an already established unit.

My profile picture has been 'super liked' by a new couple. The photo is unashamedly thirsty; I'm posing by a swimming pool in a tiny red bikini, a frosty margarita in one hand. My peroxide hair's slicked back, and my body looks – if I do say so myself – banging. Claudine, a property lawyer I used to see, took the photo on a trip we took together to Barcelona. Knowing her, she would be immensely proud if she knew that the photo she had taken had made it as my profile pic. Claudine always made everything about her.

I click on the couple's picture. Their tagline says, *Sam and Jess: married couple, looking for no-strings fun.* Their photo is very promising. Sam is a tall, handsome man, with dark skin, a shaved head, and a glorious white smile. His high cheekbones are dusted with freckles. He also has a nose piercing: not something I usually go for, but it adds to his sexiness. His wife Jess sits on top of his strong shoulders. Her chunky tanned legs are covered in tattoos; her shiny black hair is in plaits. Jess's face is heart-shaped, and her expression is crinkled into an open-mouthed giggle. They look like they're at a music festival. They look up for a laugh.

I message them:

Hey, that's me finished work for the night – how about a cocktail?

The little jumping pink dots appear to show that the other person's typing, which is my cue to place my phone into its special compartment in my handbag. I never look right away at a message. I'm not desperate, and certainly don't want to appear so.

I drive home with tunes blaring out my car. When I get into my tiny but immaculate studio flat, I feed my ragdoll cat Cardi, then check my messages. Sam and Jess have replied.

We'd love to – do you know Frankie's?

I smile. I know Frankie's; it's the best first date spot in town.

Effortlessly hipster, dark enough inside to flatter most people, and it has a brilliant cocktail menu. I frequent it so often, I'm practically on first-name terms with all the staff.

Yeah, I think so – 11pm ok?

I step out of my dress to go for a shower and take a couple pictures in the mirror of me in my black lace thong. I never waste a good photo op. The shower runs hot for a couple of minutes as I FaceTune the image and decide on an adequate filter before hitting *send.*

I pop my Betty Boop shower cap on to preserve the afternoon blow dry and style that my extensions are treated to routinely on a Friday. I shave my legs, two ways up, two ways down, and massage orange blossom scented shower oil all over my body. When I return to my room, Jess and Sam have messaged back.

Wow, can't wait to meet you IRL.

The accompanying photo is of Jess smiling cheekily, with her exposed breasts cupped by Sam's large hands. I instantly send a heart emoji back, put on some nice underwear, skinny jeans, a white vest, and re-apply my makeup. I'm not painting my face on for the back row any more, so I go for a much subtler look than before.

An hour later, I spot Sam and Jess through the window of Frankie's. They're leaning in to one another, clearly in love, which is a nice relief. I've met a few couples that obviously hadn't been vibing, and wrongly thought drafting somebody new in would help to 'spice things up'. That phrase gives me the boke. *It's a relationship, not a curry; get a grip, you losers*, I'd think, whilst pretending to receive a text about an urgent work thing, ensuring a swift exit.

Sam and Jess are now laughing heartily. Sam's knee is jiggling up and down, and when his eyes dart outside I give him a shy wave. He grins and taps the small of Jess's back; she turns around and smiles warmly at me. She's wearing horn-rimmed glasses and has a cute gap in between her teeth like old-school Madge.

I head inside and we all greet each other like old friends. The thing about three-way dates is they aren't as screamingly obvious as the ones between two people, so you can simulate an ease without everyone in the bar knowing what you're up to. Not that I really care.

They both have fresh drinks, but Sam immediately gets to his feet to go to the bar for me, leaving us girls to build an alliance: a good move on his part. I check out his shoes out of the corner of my eye. Seeing they're nice trainers, I internally breathe a sigh of relief. I cannot stand shite shoes.

'So…' Jess says, fiddling with her hair.

I notice more tattoos all up her arm, like cute little club stamps. I squeeze her leg gently. 'You alright, babe?'

'I'm a wee bit nervous,' Jess admits. Her shyness makes her even more adorable.

'No pressure; tonight can just be about getting to know you – both,' I add as Sam returns with a luminously violet Aviation for me. As he passes me my drink, my gaze goes from his wedding ring to his eyes. My stomach twists like overwrought rope.

'Well,' Sam says, addressing the bizarre nature of the situation by way of a matey toast, 'cheers!'

In the two hours at Frankie's, we talk about our jobs mostly. Sam's a theatre actor. He speaks so deliberately and confidently; I can imagine him on a stage commanding a captive audience. I admit to never having seen him in anything, but that's not surprising, because I am no theatre fan; it bores the tits right off me. We do find some common ground, however, in our careers.

He tells a hilarious story about forgetting his lines during a pantomime once, and a six-year-old girl shouting out, 'He's fucking behind you!'

I wheel out one of my best anecdotes and tell them about my worst gig, an old man's wake, where a whisky-fuelled multi-generational scrap had broken out and I was accidentally glassed in the crossfire. I show them my tiny scar, an inch from my right eye.

'Why do we put ourselves through it?' Sam laughs. 'What happened to us in childhood that meant that we had to pick jobs that require everyone to look at us and clap after we speak?'

His comment throws me off. A dad who died of cancer when I was five, and being raised by a cold and distant single mother, would be my honest answer. But honesty is not always the best policy, especially on a first date.

Jess is a palliative carer for the elderly: not as sexy as acting, but she talks with passion about the people she cares for, which is the most endearing thing. They both seem genuinely interested in me and my life: a nice plus. I field the usual first date questions about music taste and hobbies and assess that they probably don't want to murder me. That doesn't stop me from dutifully and discreetly sending a text to Anna with their names and address, from the taxi on the way to theirs. Just in case. Anna's more than a sister; she's my witness.

Their flat in the East End is a maximalist's dream. The small living room is bursting with personality, plants everywhere, patterned wall hangings and bright cushions. I make a mental note to take some selfies for Insta once we're all settled in.

As Sam's fixing us a drink, I clock the teal wall covered in a series of framed photos.

'Who is the photographer?' I ask.

'Sam,' Jess replies, fishing a packet of cigarettes out of a vintage biscuit tin and offering me one. I shake my head politely, thinking unintentionally for a microsecond about my dad, as I often do when somebody offers me a fag.

As if sensing disapproval Jess says, 'I'm quitting soon,' and shrugs apologetically, perching on the window seat and pushing the window open.

'We're going to give up all the bad stuff when we start trying for a baby,' Sam adds, passing us each a Negroni in a crystal glass. Showing a glimmer of self-consciousness, he catches himself, worrying that he's said too much.

I go to appease him straight away. 'I know what you mean. One of my pals just had a baby; you barely have time to wash!' Which is exactly why I'm never having them, I add to myself. Imagine not having time for a long soak in a bath, or an afternoon out shopping with your girlfriends. What's the point? Motherhood isn't right for everyone; my own mum is living proof of that.

I watch as Sam pushes a pair of well-loved beige Ugg slippers towards Jess and, as she instinctively slips her feet into them, I wonder what it must feel like to have somebody else know you want something even before you know yourself. I could picture them being great parents. I think to say as much but decide against it.

We sip our drinks and the conversation meanders from random topics like politics to holidays, to the elephant in the room: the app. They wonder if I've ever used it before to meet other couples.

'One or two times, yeah,' I reply breezily. No point telling them I use it on the reg.

For a moment of silence, we look amongst each other, the sexual anticipation humming just below the surface of our polite chat. It feels like we've all ordered dessert; it's yet to arrive, but we don't want the waiting staff to know that we are being impatient.

It begins, as I'd predicted, with Jess kissing me. With these delicate situations, I assume a serious conversation has been had between the couple before they met me. If we both like her, we'll bring her back? If we both really like her, Jess will make the first move?

She tastes of cigarettes and bitter orange and newness; my whole body feels on high alert to every sensation. I encourage Sam and Jess to kiss each other next; the last thing we need is anyone feeling left out before the real fun has begun.

The night goes by in a deliciously messy, hot blur. At one point the buzzer by the front door goes three times in a row, rudely interrupting us. Sam leaps off the bed, condom still on his erect penis, and storms out to answer it, a hint of impatience in his tone. Jess and I pause our kissing and giggle as we listen to him tell them off like a schoolteacher: 'It's after midnight, you know?'

When he comes back to the bed, he grabs me. His approach is like the way he speaks, every move self-assured, nothing done in haste. I like it a lot.

A satisfying score of five orgasms between us, Sam and Jess fall into a content sleep, spooning each other beside me. Their bedroom is small, but their bed is big, otherwise I would have left by now. But I'm comfortable, and I breathe in the scent of these familiar strangers. I lean over to turn the side-lamp off and notice an amateur clay ornament of two lopsided people hugging. Picking it up carefully, I read the toothpick inscription on the bottom: *For S, Love J xxx.*

I wake the following morning at the arsecrack of dawn. Stretching out, I notice my body is nice and achy: a combination of my spin workout yesterday, dancing about a stage and last night's sexual gymnastics. Once, I read an enlightening interview with a porn actress who said she felt like she'd been hit by a bus the day after shoots. I get why.

Eager not to wake Sam or Jess, I creep through to their almost egg-yolk yellow bathroom to put my jeans and vest on. Catching my quite frankly scary reflection, I shudder. I hate looking like this, bedraggled and unkempt. I carefully remove last night's makeup with some of Jess's expensive vegan face wash, finishing it off with a toner and a woody-smelling moisturiser. As I massage my face in upward circular motions, I spot their ragged his 'n' hers electrical toothbrushes sitting beside one another in the bathroom cabinet.

I tiptoe through to the living room, where the remnants of our elongated foreplay lie strewn about. My feet are cold, so I slip Jess's slippers on; they're a bit worn in, but so nice and cosy. I find my now rock-hard thong, pocket it, and chug a glass of water.

I go to rinse the glass thoroughly in the sink, and out of the window I see that the blushing sun's peeking over the glittering glass buildings of the financial district. There's plenty of time to Uber home, go for a run and then prep for the wedding gig tonight. Spring is always a busy time of year for me; it's two, three weddings a week – sometimes up to four now people have got accustomed to the Sunday wedding. If you choose to have your wedding on a Sunday, your pals will bitch about you behind your back for the inconvenience, but you're saving a grand in venue hire, so fuck them.

I think of today's bride-to-be, Christine, or Chrissy for short. She's most probably awake just now, buzzing with the excitement of the day. In a few hours she'll be drinking tea, or bubbles with her girlfriends. This could be the best day of her life.

After straightening up Jess and Sam's cushions, I take the slippers off and leave for my taxi. When I climb in, I click my seatbelt in and chirp, 'Hi, driver.'

'Good night?' the portly woman with red spiky gelled hair and gold hoops asks me in the rearview mirror.

'Aye, thanks,' I chime back.

'That's nice, hen. That's nice,' she replies, pulling out of the space.

I click the threesome app and write Jess and Sam a message:
Thanks for having me last night, you're an awesome couple
P.S. I think it's time you changed your toothbrush heads xx :)

A moment later I delete the second line, and then press *send.*

BREAK-UP

It didn't feel real for me
until I went to watch TV
and you'd changed your
Netflix password,
you bastard.

chapter 2

casual

MCCAIN

We are high on mushrooms,
fucking in the front room,
tripping out our tits.
Shit, we've burnt the chips!

CEREAL DATER

You could say
that I'm a cereal dater,
that I have a couple spoons,
then I decide that
I don't like that flavour.

But I don't see anything
wrong
with trying out
the different brands
in search of
my favourite
breakfast food
or indeed my ideal man.

I tried a bit of Corn Flakes.
He seemed like a nice guy.
We connected on
films and politics;
we both saw eye-to-eye.

Our first date was all
drinking zombie cocktails
by candlelight,
horoscopes,
childhood pets and
         Aaaaah, were you
         at that night?!
but things swiftly went tits-up
when I found out he had a wife.

Next I gave
Golden Graham a go,
but he wouldn't
get off his phone;
flicking through

social media
was where he felt
most at home.

He bored me with
dog memes
and emojis
and his constant
computer gaze.
Twelve Insta stories later,
we thankfully parted ways.

Then I got wooed
by Mr All Bran,
the older man,
the good-for-me man,
the man with a mortgage,
the man with a plan.

He chose wine
from the menu
for its region
and not its cheapness,
but his unbridled passion
for Brexit
was his big weakness.

Then I went through
a bit of a mad phase.
I started seeing a Cluster:
all-nighters,
excitement,
partying with all the
strength I could muster.

But I couldn't keep up
with his wild ways
when the parties went on
for days and days

and, sleep-deprived,
crazy-eyed and skinny,
I waved goodbye
to the maddest cereal
I ever tried.

Then I met
Jordan's Country Crisp
online.
He wore a cardigan tied
around his shoulders
and his hair smelled of
faux pine.

A picnic in the park
with quince jelly
and champagne
never swayed me.
I felt like Julia Roberts
circa *Pretty Woman*,
except he never paid me.

After him I went for a big
testosterone-oozing Weetabix,
the loudest cereal in the box,
always pontificating
and giving it big licks.

He liked an argument
and unfortunately
so did I.
The fuckboy took
my *Sopranos* boxset
and, aye, that made me cry.

Then I had a fling
with a Lucky Charm
on holiday in France.

He had the chat,
the patter,
a silver tongue;
he made me
take a chance.

But the bastard
was all talk.
I got the booby prize;
the only thing he left
me with was an effing STI.

That's what dating –
I mean
eating cereal –
is all about:
taste testing
all the bowls.
If they turn out
to be a Fruit Loop,
I'll just say Cheerio.

Maybe I'll commit
someday
to the one that
comes out on top.
Until then
I'm happy searching
for that
snap!
crackle!
pop!

FUCK

What is this?
Friends with benefits?
Benefriends?
Netflix and chill?
Penetrationship?
A fuck?
Fuck buddy?

I want to fuck you –
no, I want to be
fucked by you,
'cause fucking
is what me
and you
do best.

Let's
try anal sex,
yes,
with zero preparation
or mature discussion,
let's just do it.
I'm spontaneous;
fuck it.

Let's discuss who we fancy
with zero jealousy
or hidden agenda.
Talk to me
not about
gender inequality
or COVID-19
or the plummeting economy
or neoliberal ideologies
but low-impact
shallow stuff

like *Selling Sunset*,
wanking
or Crufts.

Fetch me
tepid tap water
in a mug
when I'm rough;
just never ever
offer to treat me
to brunch.

Breathless and sticky
twisted sheets
drunken hot
and messy
sweaty
sex with you
is the best.

Disturbed only
by the chorus of birds
outside,
and we both know
in daylight
there's less places
to hide.

In the real world
there's unopened bills,
an office job
with a dickhead boss,
and dentist's appointments.
That reminds me:
I should floss,
and it's my cousin's christening
next week.
Shit, I need to
pick up her present.

I can't believe
I almost forgot.

I like that you
don't know
my star sign
or my middle name
or even my surname
I'm guessing
judging by your demeanour
that your political leanings
are probably in keeping
with mine
but I haven't asked.

We have a laugh;
we WhatsApp
predictably
sporadically.
The chat ramps up
deliciously
every Friday
around three.

We've never
eaten a Chinese
hungover
in skanky 'jamas,
splayed
and bloated
in front of trash TV.

You've seen me
only at my best,
legs shaved, hot dress,
spanking Tesco prosecco
with reckless abandon.
Fun
flirty

happy
girl:
that's me.

There will be
no subtitled indie
movie nights,
no smelling your hair,
no peeling off
your socks
with my toes,
no petty arguments
or slamming doors,
no

WILL
YOU
PICK
YOUR
FUCKING
BOXERS
OFF
THE
FLOOR?

Don't worry,
fuck buddy,
we're cool.
I'll never fall
in love with you.

PORCH

It's the morning
after the night before.
Last night
we had conversation
after conversation;
tangents led us down
exciting rabbit holes,
jubilation,
then fornication,
and now,
now we are
here.

Now the chat feels as stale
as the overcrowded ashtray
on the floor.
The air is swimming
with a gaping awkward
silence
and the stench of
supermarket
own-brand beer.

Last night
we kissed in
the glow from your PC;
there was no awkward light
assaulting us through
unwashed windows
and chipped
cheap Ikea blinds.

Last night
was all flirty looks
and favourite books;
there was no

hangover breath
or matted hair,
no edgy stolen stares
or
damn,
I wish I'd worn
my nice underwear.

Our unfamiliar fingers
struggle
to find comfort
in the grasp
of one another's
clammy limbs.
We are odd
jigsaw pieces,
too rough
to figure out
the puzzle;
we quickly give up
on our forced
and uncomfortable
cuddle.

Last night
you were
my new best friend;
this morning
you're a stranger.
My eyes dart around
for my discarded clothing;
it's Buckarooed
to every corner
of the room,
all crumpled and dirty.
My dress has curry sauce
all down it.
Is this how it feels
to be fabulous and thirty?

You make a half-arsed excuse
about being late for work.
I try making a quick quip,
but my joke falls flat.
You gub a painkiller
and fail to muster a smirk.
I must get out of here.

As I get my shit together
I accidentally stand on your cat's tail.
I shout,
        Fuck, I'm sorry,
as Booboo lets out a wail.
(Yes, that was the cat's real name.)

There's a slight delay
as I look for my jacket.
I glance in your mirror;
geez, I'm looking pure hackett.
We rush a habitual goodbye;
you think it's a hug,
I think it's a kiss,
so we meet in the middle
with a pathetic high-five.

You mumble that you'll
give me a text or a call
when we both know
that really doesn't matter at all.
I exit with stealth
and click shut the front door,
buzzing to have escaped
from such a bore.

(Sorry, but he kept talking about cricket.)

Now my primary concern
is the location

of the nearest place
that I can get my paws
on a greasy steak bake.

But it quickly becomes apparent
that my hangover breakfast
will have to wait,
because now I'm stuck
in your porch
in a space one metre squared.
My phone's dead.
I wasn't prepared.

Panicked,
I bang
and I shout
and I scream.

But it's all in done in vain
'cause you've gone back to sleep,
so I count the tiles by my feet
and stand in there,
bored and alone,
and wait for three
and a half miserable hours
until your flatmate
eventually comes home.

SOMETHING

You are not my boyfriend.
Calling you my boyfriend
would mean it's something,
and if it's something
then when it ends
I'm left with nothing.

So it's better to say it's
nothing
than admit it's anything,
anything,
call me anything
but your girlfriend.
Let's fill in the gap between
complete strangers
and soulmates
with
something,
something like seeing.
Yes, I'm seeing you,
but if seeing is believing
does that mean
that I believe in you?

I don't believe we have a future;
it's just a bit of fun,
the type of fun
that makes me want to
hold your hand when I'm drunk,
tell you a secret,
go to you when I'm upset,
chat to my pals about you,
check my phone for your texts.

Wait, this is turning into
something,

but it's not anything.
I'm still single on Facebook
and you've not met my parents.
We are keeping this casual
because I would rather do
anything,
anything but admit
that I'm falling.

Falling suggests down,
falling suggests
face to the ground,
falling suggests
the beginning of the end,
the end of
nights out with my pals,
my independence,
any free time,
focus on my work,
spontaneity.
I mean, there's a chance
I could move abroad
any minute now,
so best not get
attached.

Attached.
We're not attached.
We're not each other's
other half.
Let's be honest:
our personalities clash,
we don't like the same tunes,
your pals are twats.

It's run its course,
so how do we break up
when we were never
really together?

Can we have a sad goodbye
when we never said forever?

Tell you what:
we'll go our separate ways,
stop hanging out
or messaging
or dating
or shagging,
OK,
and if anyone says,
        Do you know him?
I'll say yeah,
we used to have
something.

THREESOME

Thirty fingers,
thirty toes.
I'm not too sure
where everything goes.

EASY

As I push open the kitchen door, the horrendous smell hits me first. You can tell four men in their mid-twenties live here. It's like something out of a Channel 4 documentary. Trust my one-night stand to live like this. I search about for a receptacle for water and eventually settle on what looks like a small glass vase. That'll do.

Gulping my first non-alcoholic drink in twenty-fours down gratefully, I reach for the blurred memories from the previous night.

Nightclub, afters, house party, then some freezing warehouse... oh, no, wait, the house party was last. We stood in the poky living room of a barmaid called Mabel, putting stuff up our noses and talking absolute nonsense until we'd drunk the place dry. The last thing I remember having is a shot of Freball. My body shudders at the unpleasant recall.

'The thing is,' a portly guy in a sheer dress had offered, sucking on a Regal King Size that didn't stand a chance, 'Scottish people cannae be trusted to have twenty-four-hour booze shops. We're aw savages; look at the state of us!'

He wasn't wrong. I had looked around the room and taken in the almost biblical sight. A couple of scene kids in trackies were hunched over a dinner plate, snorting lines of death through a rolled-up ScotRail ticket. A lanky girl with an eccie fringe sat gurning as she painted glitter onto a sleeping man's face. He looked way older than all us, at least thirty-five, poor sod. The room had gone silent on account of the Bose speaker running out of battery some time ago. Nobody had bothered to look for the charger.

We all got chucked out soon after, something about Mabel taking her wee cousin to a theme park later. Fuck that.

The only thing I have in my calendar is work on Monday, and it's now only 4.23pm on a Saturday, which means it's still very much party time.

I spot a bottle of Lucozade lying sideways on the countertop next to a measuring tape. Its orange label glows in the daylight like a mirage. I grab it hastily, excited to taste some of the neon elixir – but it's empty.

A quick peek out of the filthy window tells me I'm in the city centre. Good, I can get the underground home when I'm done. Was the sex satisfying enough to hang around? I'm not exactly sure.

Once I went home with a guy who still lived with his parents. Feigning ease, his apron-clad mum, Sandra, insisted on cooking me and some random I'd met at the queue in Noodle King a fry-up in the morning. His dad, Bill, sat still, mostly reading the paper, but I saw the side-eye he was giving me. Trying desperately not to come off as a cheap one-night stand, I made chitter-chatter about the weather as Sandra served us over-easy eggs and cups of tea. She rambled on about the amount of rain we'd been having as I smiled politely, secretly wondering how thin the walls were and if they'd heard me getting rattled all night by their son.

Stepping out into the hallway, I concede that it's almost as bad as the kitchen. An assault course of crap lines the floor: tennis rackets, beer bottles, shoes, an old bus seat, and a rancid-smelling refuse sack waiting to be taken outside to the bins. No mum or dad to be seen, at least. The hallway leads off to five doors; which one did I come from again?

I approach one to the left of me, and hear the noises of a war video game blasting loudly. I tiptoe to the one down from that and put my ear up to it; it's quiet in there – the bathroom, maybe.

The door opposite suddenly swings open, revealing a six-foot-something man in a leopard-print dressing gown, John Lennon glasses and a giant pink cowboy hat. He has the sexiness of James Dean and the flair of Noel Fielding.

Thumping music plays from behind him on a set of decks. The current tune is an epic orchestral number, splintered by a techno beat.

For the first time since I woke up from my two-hour sleep, I'm aware that I'm wearing only a pair of unfortunately low-denier tights and an old bra; I stand feeling awkward and bony. He extends a long arm out to me, grabs my hand and pulls me into the bedroom.

Despite it being late afternoon, the blood-red curtains are pulled shut. The air is thick with incense and cigarette smoke. It's been a night that became day without anybody noticing.

'You alright?' he says in an Essex accent, giving me a crescent-moon toothy smile. On account of the sunglasses I can't see his eyes, but I sense he's smiling with them too.

'Aye,' I reply, staring up at him.

'Beautiful!' he says. I'm not sure if he means me. I doubt it. My auburn mullet's sticking to my damp, pale forehead and my eye makeup is smudged halfway down my face.

He passes me a cold can of fruit cider, and I shrug and accept it. In for a penny, in for a pound. I have a flashback of getting head in the toilets at the party and feel uncharacteristically shy. We stand in silence for a moment and then open our cans in unison.

'Peace and love,' he says slowly, reading the letters from the stick-and-poke designs that cover my knuckles on both hands.

('That won't age well, you know,' Granny Margo had said when I showed her them.

'Good,' I replied. 'Neither will I.'

'No use telling you what to do because you'll do exactly what you want to do anyway, won't you?' she said with resignation, sipping her G&T.)

Knowing my dress is in a crumpled heap and probably honking I ask, 'Do you have a shirt or something I can wear?' I pause. 'Also what's your name?'

'Leo.' He laughs and then sucks in his breath. 'How about yours?'

'Florence,' I say, smiling. Maybe I'll hang around for a bit.

I take a drink of the sickly sweet cider. The bubbles gather like gossipy fishwives in my empty stomach. It gargles, but the music's too loud for Leo to hear.

He looks me up and down and sweeps over to an exposed clothes rail in the corner of the room. He rifles through the items for a minute or two, glancing back at me once or twice. Eventually he settles on a baby pink floor-length sheer nightgown with feathered sleeves.

I slip it on and immediately feel like a movie star from yesteryear, one who drinks on the job and takes multiple lovers.

I mean, that's who I am now, to be fair… minus the movie star bit. Leo passes me a pair of heart-shaped rose-tinted glasses and I complete the look.

He marches me over to the full-length mirror that's covered in peeling skateboarding stickers and he stands behind me. We look like a couple who would get barred for trashing a hotel room. I would chuck a telly out of a window with him any day.

We dance along to the tune together until it reaches the end. Leo jumps over to the decks and puts another record on, bobbing his head instinctively to the beat.

'Why don't you take your glasses off?' I coax him.

He slowly removes them, revealing cartoon-like, shiny, sleep-deprived eyes.

He puts his hands on the back of my neck; his fingers feel long and cold, and slightly clammy. I feel safe and scared.

'You know something? You are a bit of alright,' he says.

'What do you mean?' I let my gown fall open slightly. He looks at me for a long time, and his hands release me as he sways to the music.

I reach into my bra to peel off a little white baggy that had been melded to my left nipple and wave it at him. He grins.

Our connection flourishes like one of those sped-up videos of a Livingstone daisy at dawn. He is the sun and I am a sexy little flower.

We take line after line after line. He puts on record after record. We drink can after can.

Blurry and jaggy, in his company, I feel alive. We dance and talk meaningfully about meaningless shit. And then we kiss. His lips are cracked and dry and my tongue pushes inside his mouth to find answers.

And with that slow long kiss, I'm in love. Just like that. Well, at least I think I am. I feel I am. Maybe it's the coke or cider, but maybe it's not. Maybe this is the beginning of something truly amazing.

But the kiss stops with the sudden feeling we are being watched.

I break away from Leo's strong hold and look to see a short bulldog of a man with a sizeable tribal tattoo snaking up his chest. He wears baggy gym shorts and a look of disgust.

He is the person I went home with last night.

Eventually, I gesture to the white-dusted Reservoir Dogs DVD case and say, with the strained, polite tone of an air stewardess at the end of her rope, 'Line?'

EMPTY TRACKIE

He tossed me about
like an empty trackie jacket,
crunched me up
like an old crisp packet,
spread me thin like Lurpak
on burnt toast,
abandoned me to stew
like a Sunday pot
roast,
left me hollow
like a bog roll tube,
crushed me
between his teeth
like a big ice cube.

He put me out
like a fag dout,
halted sex
mid-flow
to put on a bet,
refused to wear
a condom,
his bedroom was a
capharnaum,
told me he'd
pay me back,
talked shit
behind my back,
laughed
when he left
a red handprint
on my left bum cheek,
didn't text me
for almost two
whole weeks.

So why
does my heart sing
every time
my phone goes ping?

UTI

It stings as she urinates,
feels like fucking
razor blades
have declared war
on her urethra.

She lets out a muffled cry
into the elbow
of the oversized
nineties rock band T-shirt
that she wears as
a makeshift
nightie;
hungover from last night's
overindulgence in white wine
out a box,
she's trying
not to whitey.

As her free hand holds
on to the side of the sink,
her thumb squidges into a
hardened blob
of white and pink
ignored Colgate.
She hisses
          fuck's sake
and her painted toes curl
on the unmopped floor.
Meanwhile
he jovially whistles
the theme tune of
Peep Show
next door.

He's a graphic designer
skinny,
into indie,
loves Stephen King,
a wee bit kinky.
He's sound enough
and he makes her laugh,
but since the start of their fling
she's had so many issues
in her pants:
pH imbalance,
cystitis,
thrush,
BV.

> *Why does sex with him*
> *cause all these problems with me?*

After several more
agonising minutes of
wincing and
urging burning pee
to leave
her body
less antagonistically,
she wipes and sees
remnants of red.
She climbs back into bed
and he passes her a lit fag and says,

> *That was some shag!*

She nods,
making a mental note
to pick up cranberry juice
on the way home.

EX-GIRLFRIEND

We used to pick out fancy wine.
She taught me how to sixty-nine.
Now when I see her
on my walk home
I pretend to be on my phone.

Chapter 3

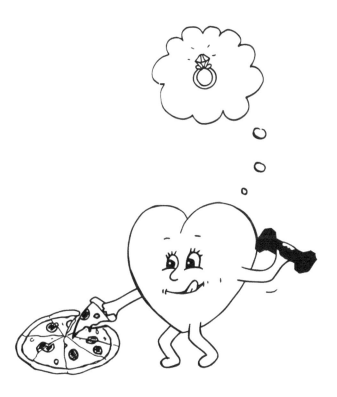

wanting

HEN DO: HOME EDITION

Never have I ever
been fingerblasted
on a Megabus.
I take a
self-conscious gulp
as the room goes hushed.
Supermarket bubbles
fizz down my throat.
The mother of the bride
looks horrified
and asks,
        Is that meant to be a joke?

ORLA

How could someone have grown up around an unlimited supply of free biscuits and cakes and still look like the side of a fiver? I wondered as Gareth belched loudly and clawed at an Asda paper plate of misshapen shortbread.

He lived upstairs in my block at halls, and today was his eighteenth birthday. His throw-enough-shit-at-the-wall approach to invitations meant that the soulless living room was rammed full of first-years, basking in their newfound freedom.

Gareth was a waif-like, gormless heir to a mammoth confectionary company in the Highlands. His parents had couriered him an obscene quantity of factory-rejected treats for the party. A group of people beside me were slugging vodka straight from the bottle, a custom they would soon come to realise never reaped positive results. They were singing along unironically to pop music. Back when pop music was decent. The questions 'What school did you go to?' and 'What Highers did you get?' floated in the air like a bad stench. I circuited the fringes of the party, feeling like one of those gingerbread people with no head.

Finding a square of bristly carpet in the corner of the room, I pretended to fill myself up with a drink from the optics – another gift from Gareth's parents – trying desperately not to look as socially awkward as I felt. We were in our third week of first year and I felt as shy as I did on my very first day. The hum of not fitting in got louder with every tutorial; each lecture sitting by myself was further evidence that I was destined to be alone forever. I observed the birthday boy as he strawpedoed his fifth orange alcopop and petulantly launched a piece of birthday cake across the room at some unsuspecting party guests.

'Who the fuck flung that at me?' a Belfast voice boomed over the latest Nelly Furtado tune that was pounding out of the bile-coloured iPod speaker. The voice belonged to Orla Doherty. She was a five-foot-nothing firecracker. A mountain of angry red hair was piled on top of her elfin face, her green eyes imprisoned by smudged kohl, making her look like a sexy cartoon raccoon. She had the type of face that spidery mascara trails would not look out of place on. A smirk lurked behind her mouth, like a confidently quiet teenage boy at a wedding, waiting for his parents to turn their backs so he could steal a cheap bottle of wine.

A chubby and prematurely balding second-year in skinny jeans with floppy hair and guyliner on tripped over me. 'Shorreeee, dude': he offered a slurred apology. Orla spotted me, held up a cigarette and a lighter and cocked her head, signalling for me to follow her outside. I wasn't a smoker, but anything would be better than this.

We wandered across the bridge over the filthy canal together. Orla gently pulled the conversation along, talking about the party, and about scoring weed off a guy called Elvis who she clearly thought was a bit of a fanny. I nodded in sage acknowledgment as if I knew who he was. I found myself clambering for fun and interesting things to say. With a sad resignation, I knew that it was in panicked moments like these that my mind would suddenly go blank and fail to come up with anything at all.

Orla said she'd seen me about uni. I couldn't imagine anybody would notice me, with my impotent mousey brown bob and safe Primark outfits, but I felt tickled by her words nonetheless.

We walked to an old man's pub down the road. The frosted windows had grime-covered grids over them, like dirty chip pans. Orla opened the door and gestured for me to go first. When I walked in, the smell of beer breath, cheese and onion crisps and body heat hit me like drunken snog.

We found a wonky table by the dartboard and pretended to ignore the stares from a dozen pot-bellied men. 'They're acting like they've never seen an emo before,' Orla laughed.

She ordered a Malibu and Coke, and I got a Long Vodka. It was a drink I'd only recently become accustomed to; I felt it was less of a commitment than a pint and far more mature than what that lot were all drinking at Gareth's party.

'Two tequilas as well,' I chirped at the bleached-haired barmaid, who looked like she could single-handedly batter every customer in here. She looked between us, popped her chewing gum like a gunshot and asked for our ID in a raspy monotone.

'Who brings a passport out?' Orla teased when I handed the barmaid mine. 'Where's your driving licence?'

'I don't have one. I couldn't aff— I couldn't be bothered.' I felt my face betray me by going red.

'Oh, me too, I just have a provisional. I was more fussed about my dancing, sure.' She smiled.

'What kind of dancing?' I asked, impressed.

The barmaid slammed two oily, clear tequilas in front of us. No salt or lime, and the look on her face told us not to bother asking for some either.

Orla's eyebrows arched, like seductive jet-black caterpillars. 'Flamenco,' she said, deadpan. On seeing my surprise she added, 'I'm joking – Irish.'

We slung the shots back, pretended not to hate the taste, paid, then carried our drinks to the pokey table we had claimed with our jackets. Orla told me all about her life before uni; she was a competitive dancer.

She gestured animatedly with her hands, which were adorned with chunky silver rings and finished off with chipped black nail polish. I couldn't take my eyes off her. Was she real? This quick-witted, charming, pixie dream feminist badass. So far, everyone I had met at uni had, either subconsciously or consciously, let me know that I wasn't meant to be in their gang. And I agreed with them. The pretty cheerleaders, the ecstasy-munching techno crew, the annoyingly extroverted theatre kids, the indie lot with their androgynous hair and snooty music tastes.

'You'll find your cuppa tea,' my dad had said, before I left for my new grey and unwelcoming home. I felt guilty that he was working two jobs just to afford my rent here. And he was meaning to be supportive, but when he kept saying, 'You're the first to go to uni, hen; knock 'em dead,' all I felt was pressure. Orla and I got pissed. We took turns to buy rounds, one time with the added rush of a tequila, the other with a couple of bags of crisps. Orla expertly tore them open so we could share the two flavours. What a pro.

Before we knew to even look at the time, the barmaid rang a big brass bell, signalling last orders. 'Doesn't matter how old we are, whether we're in school or the pub, we always need a bell telling us it's time to go home,' Orla remarked as we left, the cool air kissing our rosy cheeks.

We linked arms all the way home, apart from when I challenged her to show me some of her dancing. Rather than pretend to be shy, she immediately handed me her black studded handbag and leapt across the pavement, her fishnet-covered legs nimbly moving around at an incredible speed; her Vans trainers were blurred under her as she bounced from side to side. When she finished, glowing and breathless, a hunched guy across the road in a cap shouted nasally, 'That was amazin', darlin'!'

And I agreed. We arrived giggling and clumsy back at my flat. Music was still blaring from Gareth's floor.

'Shall we go back to the party?' I asked wryly.

'I've seen enough fannies for one night,' Orla quipped as I buzzed us in with my fob.

I didn't know where to look when she got undressed. To give her some privacy, I turned my back, coming face-to-face with my beige wall. I kicked myself internally for not having something more exciting than my term one timetable up. My face burned at the neon pink and yellow highlighter I'd used to indicate the different subjects; it suddenly felt so juvenile. Dad had bought them for me as part of my leaving-for-university package. My heart panged at him in his hi-vis, walking into WH Smith or The Works, absolutely clueless. He probably asked the sales assistant for help; no chance he'd picked out those heart-shaped Post-it notes and embossed writing pads himself. At the time I was delighted; I loved stationery. But now it felt childish. I made a mental note to redo my timetable in something cooler. Like a fountain pen.

When I turned round, Orla was standing on my bed, putting a sock over the smoke alarm with the deftness of someone who had done it many times before. Her arms were stretched up, the T-shirt I had lent her riding up to her knickers. She winked at me before stepping off the bed.

As she sat cross-legged on the floor rolling a joint, I frantically scrolled through my second-hand scratched iPod Touch to find some music that wasn't completely embarrassing. I settled on a YouTube playlist called *After the Club*. Orla lit the joint and, shiny eyelids half shut, took a long drag. She handed it to me and, copying her, I did the same.

'You into boys or girls, by the way?' she asked through the smoke rings she had made with her expert exhalation. As the new sensation of smoke filling my lungs hit me, I started to choke. I gestured for her to hand me yesterday's glass of water from next to my bed.

As I gulped it down and spluttered, Orla rubbed my back.

'Maybe we don't need this.' She rolled the end of the joint on my outer window ledge until the glow was gone and placed it on my desk.

My head felt extremely fuzzy, although not, I observed, in a bad way.

'Should we go to bed?' I asked her. I'd never asked anybody that before.

Orla nodded and crawled in first, her wild hair sprawled over my pillow, making itself at home. I hastily changed into my pyjamas and climbed in beside her, hiding under the crisp polka dot bed covers.

The room was spinning with possibility.

She twisted around and backed into me, melding us into the spooning position. Her hair tickled under my nose. Rigid at first, I relaxed into the shape of her. I closed my eyes and saw barmaids and bells ringing and tequilas.

'Both,' I whispered as we fell into a stoned sleep together. 'I'm into both.'

GIRL AT MY GYM

Girl at my gym,
you are narrow-waisted,
pert-chested,
thick and slim
in all of the right places.
You wear tiny little tops
that show off your killer abs.
If I had to take a stab
I'd say that you
must work in fashion.

That would explain
those designer leggings,
or, judging by the
massive glittering rock
on your finger,
maybe you
have a loaded fiancé?

You have the presence
of someone who knows
that she is bang tidy.
We all know the vibe,
head held real high.

Your journey
to the water fountain
is a strut worthy
of a London Fashion Week
catwalk.
Your long blonde hair swishes
from side to side
as you trot on the treadmill.
You are a show pony.

No matter how much you train,

you never
break into a bead of sweat,
you're never out of breath,
your contoured
perfectly makeup-caked face
never even goes pink,
let alone red.

Your toned arms
are a St Tropez brown;
no streaks, of course.
You and your man must
own one of those second homes.

Your life is just a long string
of holidays
like clothes on a washing line
punctuated by posh brunches,
skinny lattes
with your equally hot pals,
spa weekends,
bank-breaking cocktails
in high-end bars.
Tenner's bet
your dog
is better dressed than me.

You've clearly never left a bog
with your skirt
tucked into your thong
or bumped into your ex
the day your fringe
was cut wrong.

Or queefed during sex
or sent an accidental text
to your boss
calling him
a shady shit-munching prick.

Everything is perfect for you.
I can tell
that you're not
in credit card hell,
you don't still live
with your folks.

You're not doing far less
than your best
to sell central heating
over the phones,
stuffing your puss
with Domino's
in the evenings,
eating your feelings,
guzzling cheap vino
to try and forget
that you won't ever be
your ideal weight
and you'll never escape
from your debt.
No, your hardest decisions are
what shade of paint
to use in your dining room,
dove's tail or elephant's breath,
or where you should next invest.

You like it when
your husband does
the talking,
you drink champagne
when you go
midweek shopping,
you own multiple cars
and you can always
find a parking space,
even in Shawlands.

Do you know what?
You have inspired me.
From now on
I'm going
to do intense workouts:
cardio
weights
strength
burpees
sit-ups
squats
the lot.
You'll see me at that gym
every single day,
but
starting tomorrow,
'cause it's two-for-one Tuesday.

BAT CAVE

We're sat in the corner,
drinking cider
from Sports Direct mugs
and chewing the fat.
Your fingers
are spinning a Zippo lighter.

I'm mesmerised
as you sit
and it flips
on your lap.
You're telling a story;
I'm not quite sure what it's about,
but my face hurts from laughing
at the chat you can spout.

Gurning lips
meet filter tips;
your laugh's making
my stomach flip.
Your mate
just offered me a trip.
I shake my head
and take a sip.

Through fag smoke haze
I meet your gaze,
lock eyes with you,
then look away.
It's going to be one of those days
full of reckless fun mistakes.

Table salt absorbs
puddles of red wine,
pals play-fight
and strangers cuddle,
a noisy girl sings

slightly out of time,
wee groups of
nose-to-table huddles,
rips in tights,
talking shite,
        Mate... you got a light?
Sunlight creeps
under the blind.

        Does anyone have the fucking time?

The offy's gonna open any time;
everyone knows it's carryout time.
        Here,
        can you buy me two bottles of wine?

No point us all going;
just give him cash,
check my bag
for the usual smash.
You smile at me.
        Let's get smashed.
The next few hours
go by in a drunken flash;
some folk in the party
begin to crash.

Makeup's abandoned
for bathroom debates;
we interlock fingers
and you say,
        It's getting late.

Arms round one another,
we fall deep in conversation.
You even kiss me lightly
on my mascara-stained cheek.
My body fizzes
in anticipation

from our flirtation;
it looks like we're going to…
but then the buzzer beeps.
Everyone's quiet.

     Who is it?
The atmosphere shifts
when someone whispers,
     Polis.
We hear people talking in the hallway,
strain to make out what they're saying.

Then the door slams shut;
they've invited the person in.
People scramble
to cover dusty mirrors
and personalised weed tins,
the tunes are turned right off,
nobody utters a word.
Then a gorgeous
leggy
redhead
walks in and you say,

     I'd like you to meet my bird!

CHEMICALS

We met on a work's night out.
Please picture the scene:

pleather karaoke booths,
a free bar,
avoiding eye contact
with Gill from HR,
an untouched buffet
of beige Farmfoods,
finger food,
did I mention the free bar?

The dimly lit room is filled
with about twenty millennials
who hate working
at that call centre
almost as much
as they love getting on it.

A wobbly rendition
of an eighties classic is belted out
unashamedly
by Baz from accounts,
and with just one look
me and my relatively handsome
workmate escape.

Booze floods through
our bloodstreams
as we talk about everything,
caught up in a whirlwind,
shot with an arrow
by a cock-eyed Cupid.
He
is just the tonic for me;
the alchemy

of it all
makes me giddy.
Guard was up to begin with,
but with him it melts away
pretty quickly;
see, to be honest,
I'm defenceless
to his charms
disarmed
by bevvy-laden banter,
patter delivered to me
by a supreme enchanter.

We meet up
the very next day:
our first official date.
It's a far too summery
Saturday in May.
Glasgow's absolutely cooking.

We get steamboats
in an overcrowded beer garden.
He says
we're lucky to get a spot.
I just feel lucky
that I'm with him.
We are the bubbles
in Tennent's tops
and ethanolic whisky chasers
on the rocks,
and on the sly
I text my bestie,
omg I think I love him
<3 <3 <3

We're swept up
as sunset drives us to a
friendly dispute
in an auld man's pub.

The usual clientele
roll their eyes at
the loud snort in my laugh,
but I don't give two hoots.
We end up
at the dancing that night,
and in the smoking area
our faces are pink and freckled
from the unanticipated sun
and our skin is sweaty
and I'm so happy,
and back inside
over the music I shout,
        This is so much fun!

I know
I'm a fanny.

And then
the perfect storm
of
dopamine
oxytocin
nicotine
adrenaline
serotonin
and whatever
the fuck we got
that fucked us up
so much.

I'm romanced
by his quick-witted chat
outside that shitty nightclub
and then back
at the afterparty
at that student flat
where we play Twister
and FaceTime his wee sister.

And he
is full of philosophy
and academic musings
and we dance
to unironic nineties RnB
on repeat
'til the sun comes up
and
falling in love
out your nut
is some buzz.

WATER SIGN

Some people spring out of bed in the morning, start their day with a spot of meditative yoga, or a nice artisan coffee as they sit by their French windows and prepare their itemised to-do lists. I am not one of those people. Today I plan to smoke at least two doobies, masturbate furiously to photos of Paul Mescal and eat a share bag of Doritos in bed – in exactly that order.

It's called self care. I'm shattered from four long nursing shifts in a row at the hospital. Cleaning bed sores, taking temperatures and chasing distracted dickhead doctors to administer fluids sure takes it out of you.

I groggily look under my pillow for my lighter and spark a joint. My first delectable draw is interrupted by my flatmate Romik chapping my bedroom door.

'Come in, Ro!' I shout, exhaling smoke sideways and wiping sleep from my eye.

He shuffles in, careful not to step on the giant heap of clothes that I've left by the door. Romik's a second-generation Glaswegian Indian, just below average height, and, with a chiselled face and short black beard, he's objectively handsome. It's hard to be objective when he's wearing a Simpsons dressing gown, a present gifted to him three birthdays ago from his overbearing mum.

'This is where you keep your dirty laundry?' He blinks through his thick black-rimmed glasses at me.

'How dare you, it's clean!' I hold the joint out as an offering, knowing full well he'll say no, but it's fun to wind him up.
He wrinkles his nose and tightens his robe before saying, gravely, 'Jade, our boiler's broken.'

Romik and I met when we were two idiot students working at a cowboy-themed restaurant. We served cheeseburgers with names like Buffalo Billy Connolly to rowdy tables of pished stag do's. If being in the trenches of a shite hospitality job doesn't bond you inexplicably to another human being in the same position, then I don't know what will.

'Pour us another pint, Ro,' I would slur at our inevitable lock-ins every night, my arm looping around his neck like an unwanted necklace that he couldn't bring himself to take off.

About eight months ago, Romik's toxic girlfriend Ailsa had dumped him for the third time in a year, just as a room in my two-bed flatshare became available. Finally taking everybody's advice, he thankfully decided he was no longer standing for her bullshit and moved in with me. The only thing worse than living with your own heartache is sharing a flat with someone who is experiencing it themselves. I'm no expert in relationships – most of mine fizzle out around the six-month mark – but I happen to know a lot about break-ups. I nursed him the Jade way. Booze, scary movies, pizza and more booze.

Admittedly, after the initial honeymoon period wore off, our cohabiting came as bit of a shock to both of our systems. His obsession with order and tidiness baffles me as much as my messiness irritates him. A successful sports physio, Romik finds safety in boring things like logic, routine and folding his clothes a specific way. He works out every evening at the exact same time and plans his dinners down to the last boring boiled broccoli floret. I'm more of a 'see what I feel like eating and then order it from Just Eat' kind of gal.

'Do we have boiler cover?' I ask sleepily. Unfortunately, we both know the answer to that question because it was me who was meant to sort it.

Romik chooses not to point this out. 'I filled the bath with water from the kettle,' he says instead.

'How long did that take you?' I ask through a gaping wide yawn. I don't bother to cover my mouth, and I see him try not to flinch.

Romik replies matter-of-factly, 'About twenty minutes.'

I flick a tiny bit of ash into an old can of Irn-Bru and consider the effort. I'm tired even thinking about the prospect of having to boil our kettle repeatedly.

'Maybe I'll just jump in your bathwater. Did you shower at the gym last night?'

'Yes. I'm not an animal,' he replies.

When I go into the bathroom, I notice that he's wiped the sink and mirror clean and straightened up the products that line the bath. How can he be fucked? I dip myself into the lukewarm water and slosh some bath soak in, cycling it into a second gasp of frothy bubbles. I remember how much I used to love taking baths. I'm a Scorpio, which is a water sign, so that makes sense. Romik's a Virgo, an earth sign. He scoffs every time I mention any of this 'woo-woo' stuff to him, but that's typical Virgo (with a Capricorn moon) behaviour if you ask me.

The ground-floor Glasgow tenement we're renting shows its age by refusing to heat up, even with an electric heater blasting. Romik notes how much the leccy bill's going to be with it on all the time too, but I ignore him. An engineer comes round and, as he loudly slurps on an instant coffee with a 'coo and two', he tuts and says the boiler is well and truly 'pan breid'.

That night we sit in the kitchen, wrapped in hoodies and scarves. Romik's on cooking duties, which is a blessing for both of us. My attempt at making an asparagus risotto for a dinner party once was so cataclysmically bad that the story has gained legendary status in our household.

'Wine?' I ask as he delicately serves up two heavenly-smelling bowls of spag bol. The steam from it curls up in the air and I breathe it in gratefully. Usually, when I offer him wine on a school night, he declines. 'It'll warm you up,' I add cheekily.

'I'll try anything tonight. It's so cold, my balls have retracted into my body,' he says dryly.

It's so weird; until this moment, I never thought of Romik as having sexual organs before. Before, I wouldn't have been surprised if he'd pulled down his trousers and all that was there was a Ken doll style smooth mound.

Buzzing to have a drinking buddy, I fill two chipped B&M wine glasses from a bottle of our corner shop's finest and we toast to getting a new boiler 'as soon as fucking possible'.

One bottle turns into two, which leads to a game of ours: Human Jukebox. Taking it in turns, we pick a song each, with each one receiving a 'yasss' or a 'aw, belter'. The night reaches a crescendo when I whap on my pièce de resistance: the cheesy track that the cowboy-themed restaurant had on repeat. Romik hugs me goodnight. He's so fun when he's half-cut.

The following night is Friday, but, feeling mildly hungover, I cancel my drinks with my work pals. I end up, by default, having a movie night with Romik, so we sit on an hand-me-down Chesterfield couch with beers and snacks.

The second film we picked out together is a Japanese horror, and for every jump scare or gory bit I instinctively grab on to Romik's arm in terror. One time, my grip stays on his forearm for a little too long. I snap it back, dipping it into the popcorn for something to do.

I'm not sure why, but saying goodnight is slightly awkward tonight, and I listen to the familiar creaks and clicks of Romik's bedtime routine with more of an invested interest than before. I can't seriously be developing a crush on Romik, can I?

The next morning, a gloomy, grey Saturday, I emerge from my room to see him fetching the vacuum cleaner out of the hall cupboard. He looks all clean and fresh, his short, dark hair erect on his head, microdroplets of water clinging on to it. He also smells great, and the intimacy of knowing we use the same shower gel makes me feel oddly shy.

'How long ago did you wash? Have I missed bath time?' My flirty attempt at a joke comes out as an infantilised huff. Romik puts the vacuum down.

'Why don't you head in and I'll top you up?' he offers.

I'm not sure what else to say but yes, and I head into the bathroom, leaving the door ajar. After removing my pyjamas, I fold them neatly and place them on the radiator, pretending for once that I am that type of person, conscientious and tidy. The type of person Romik would appreciate.

There are remnants of bubbles, but certainly not enough to cover what needs to be covered, so, when he brings the kettle through, he's sure to avert his eyes from my naked body. I hide my bits under a floating sponge just in case.

Romik knocks the door gently, then approaches the edge of the bath. I curl up my feet to avoid being scalded. He pours the kettle into the tub and the welcome embrace of heat reaches in between my legs first.

'Thanks, Ro,' I whisper.

'No worries.' He leaves the room, clicking the door shut.

That night I go out for drinks with my two besties Shonagh and Tegan. We sit in our noisy local, squealing as we peer over pictures of the new man that Tegan's dating, an older gentleman from Edinburgh.

'His cock is huge, and he can go for hours,' Tegan brags as her long talons swipe through a selection of photos.

Dating has become something of a sport amongst us. We always give nicknames to the men we're dating: Car Wash Guy, Radio Guy, Wine Guy, Thumb Guy, Mullet Guy, Neighbour Guy etc. Tegan's man de jour is dubbed Silver Guy, for obvious reasons.

Tegan tries to skip past it, but I spot a photo of Silver Guy at an aquarium with two young children. 'He probably lasts so long because he pops Viagra; he's an actual OAP. He still puts Facebook albums up, for Christ's sake,' I quip. 'Is that his grandkids in that one?'

Tegan pulls her phone back and shoves it into her Prada bum bag huffily. That's right: a Prada bum bag. Shonagh's spotted it at the same time as me; she grabs the bag and inspects it in wonder.

'Is this real?' Her mouth gapes open.

Tegan swipes it back like it's her firstborn. 'Yes, it is,' she huffs. 'And what?'

Shonagh and I exchange a triumphant look. A look that says, *Silver Guy isn't a good ride; he's just minted!*

'At least I'm getting a regular shag the now,' Tegan jabs at me. 'How is life as a born-again virgin?'

Shonagh betrays me with a nasal snort.

'It's been four and a half months; it's hardly closed over,' I shoot back defensively.

Later that night, alone in the kitchen and high on sugary cocktails, I stand impatiently by the kettle, watching the steam penetrating the air with gusto as it boils for my hot water bottle. I grab an old newspaper from the kitchen table and clatter about for a pen before scrawling a drunken note, leaving it by the kettle.

In the morning, I wake up dry-mouthed and groggy, and I am suddenly gripped with a cold, sweaty fear. Rushing through to the kitchen, I try to find the note, but it's gone. It's a sickening realisation that Romik must have seen it and read these excruciating words:

Why don't we have a bath together in the AM? xxx

I may have been drunk, but I remember that I had underlined the word *together* three times. I feel sick. I scuttle back through to my bedroom and in my haste trip over one of last night's trainers. Fuck my life.

Crawling back into my bed, I scramble for ideas of how to play it. Denial? Grovel? Make a joke? Pretend I was winding him up? I immediately text my group chat, looking for advice, but Shonagh and Tegan are both asleep.

I hear a door, and a creak, and a… fuck, he's up. My blood runs colder than the air in my bedroom. Romik comes charging through and looks, for lack of a better word, furious.

'Are you fucking kidding me, Jade?'

'What?' I tighten my duvet around me.

'You can't be leaving me notes like this,' he says, flinging the newspaper on the pile of washing. I spot a pair of scrubs with a questionable stain on them. Maybe that's the dirty pile after all.

'I'm sorry. If it helps… I meant it?'

'You meant it? You can't go around asking your pals to share baths with you; have you lost the plot?'

Sensing this is a rhetorical question, I remain quiet.

He continues. 'Sex is obviously one big joke to you, isn't it? Blind date this, one-night stand that. Well, that's not me. It means a lot to me when I sleep with a girl. It's not just some funny anecdote that I can laugh about afterwards.'

'Right, so I'm a big slag?' I find myself shouting. 'At least I don't let people treat me like shit. You think going out with someone like Ailsa is better than playing the field? At least I respect myself.'

'Sure!' Romik smirks and gestures around my room.

That's it. I leap off the bed and suddenly feel the need to shove him. I take myself by surprise when I do it, two hands smacking up against his hard chest. He grabs my wrists. We look at each other's ugly anger.

Then Romik says measuredly, 'You leave every single kitchen cupboard open when you're cooking. Not to mention the food you make is barely edible. Your dishes are left in the sink under the guise of needing soaked. Every plughole in the flat is full of your frizzy hair. At weekends your shoes decorate the hallway like a surprise assault course. You leave doors unlocked and candles burning and…'

I stare up at him, my heart pounding like a gabba beat.

He continues, 'I tolerate every single one of your chaotic ways. Because you're funny, and warm, and you are the only thing that's made me smile since…'

'So fine,' I say. 'Let's have a bath together.'

And so this is how I have found myself, at 2pm on a Sunday in January, drinking beers in a bath with my flatmate, with his big toe up my vagina. Romik removes his glasses, which have steamed up. It makes him look comically unthreatening. He folds them carefully and places them on the side of the sink, continuing to rock his foot gently back and forth. His strong, sculpted thighs dip in and out of the soap suds, whilst his soft hands run up the sides of my legs. I tip my head back and dunk my masses of curls under the water, writhing in pleasure. When I emerge from the water, I take a long sip from my beer.

Romik removes his foot from in between my legs and we both lean in for a sloppy, hunched, glorious kiss. The juxtaposition of familiarity and newness is like trying an espresso martini for the first time.

'You're not so easy to live with yourself,' I tell Romik as he breaks the kiss, holding my hair in his fists. Have we fancied each other all this time? Definitely not. I've seen him crying his eyes out over his ex, stuffed up and snotty with man flu, seething over an incorrect phone bill, arguing with his dad about tennis, hungover, tired, grumpy. I've seen all the bits you usually put up with because you are in love. Not to mention all that he's seen of me. Bringing back a Tinder date who was a full foot shorter than me and kept calling me Jane. My terrible mood swings when I'm on my period. How I eat with my mouth full and sometimes smoke in bed, and how I forget to clean up after myself, let's face it, all the time. He's seen every ugly corner of me, and yet he still wants to kiss my face off! When it starts as friendship, does love find ways to exist in the spaces around all that?

The hot kissing goes on until the bath is ice-cold. Romik climbs out first and holds a towel up for me. I step into it gratefully with as much dignity as I can muster. My teeth are beginning to chatter. I can't wait to climb into bed and feel his body heat against mine.

'I'll grab us another beer,' I offer, shuffling across the freezing wooden floor to the kitchen, like an emperor penguin.

When I stride into his bedroom, Romik's staring at his mobile phone. I left my towel on the kitchen floor, figuring I wouldn't be needing it anyway.

'Hey, sexy!' I purr, my hair wet and sprawling, and my usually tanned face flushing with excitement. But something has changed. Romik's face looks different. I know that look. He gets it whenever she messages him. Ailsa.

There's a humiliating moment of silence, as I stand before him, my fanny out, holding two beers like a tool.

He finally speaks, quietly and low. 'Maybe this was a mistake. Sorry, Jade.'

BLOW JOB

You can ask,
you can beg,
but if you push my head
I'll kick your baws instead.

SOME GIRLS

Some girls are growing up
in a world
where *feminism* is a dirty word.
We are bound by heteronormative
ideology:
live and act a certain way,
it's part of your biology.

Advertisers will prey
on your every insecurity.
After all,
there's endless opportunities
for them to capitalise
on your low self-worth.
Your value will come from
how good a selfie
you can take of your bum
and how much you
can suck in your tum
for a photo uploaded
to Instagram.

You'd better
pluck
and shave
and dye
and starve yourself
as much as you can
in your endless search
to find a man,
otherwise
I'd be surprised
if Prince Charming
gave you a second glance.

It's better to romanticise
than to criticise
while you wait to be saved,
and remember
that, if you ever get raped,
if you happened to be drunk
or wearing a short skirt
then it's you
who'll get the blame.

And if you dare express
a need for sex
then you'd best expect
to be belittled
and shamed,
catcalled and trolled,
called a slut,
a slag,
a tramp
or a whore.

Please don't forget
that the most important
part of your body
is your mind.
Besides being hot
you can be strong
and brave
and intelligent
and kind.

Let's stop putting
our wee yins in boxes,
pink or blue,
Barbies or trucks.
Why not just
teach them equal respect
and love and trust?
Show that boys can be caring
and girls can be tough.

There's binary codes
that we could reject;
all they do is limit,
restrict and oppress.
Don't let anyone dictate
how you behave,
think or dress.

Look beyond this
vacuous trash,
forget
     girls are too soft
and
     lads will be lads,
be the best person
you can possibly be,
stick two fingers up
to the patriarchy.

HEN DO: ABROAD EDITION

Take us to Casa Del smfijvir!
she slurs to the bemused taxi driver,
a Bride 2 Be sash wrapped around her,
waving a crumpled sterling fiver.

chapter 4

missing

I DON'T MISS YOU

I don't miss
your tyrannosaurus snores,
your work uniform
in an abandoned heap
on the floor.

I'm no
longer forced
into complete boredom
watching football,
engaging
in your pointless fandom;
no more
pretending that I care
when your team wins.
Now I have more time
for all of my hobbies.

I joined the gym.
I'm getting slim.
It's not
the break-up diet,
I swear.
I got a septum piercing.
I dyed my hair.
I tell myself,
    My life is just better off without him.

I don't miss your smell
and how you liked
to use ladies' shower gel,
you big
coconut-and-jasmine-infused prick.

I don't miss your coo's lick
and those lines by your mouth

that appear
when you make a sarcastic joke
and the way you used to stroke
my hair behind my ears.

I don't miss
getting stoned out of our tits,
sitting on our tattered couch
listening to techno
and eating fish finger butties,
passing tommy sauce,
inexpertly discussing
conspiracy theory
documentaries.

Admittedly,
unfortunately,
for me
there is a void
in my thoughts
in most situations,
every conversation:
a missing space,
a black hole.
Truthfully
I don't know
how to be
just me,
but I would like to believe that
one day soon
I'll say
I don't miss you
and it will be true.

THURSDAYS

Thursdays
are my favourite day.
We both finish work,
him at the office and
me at the café,
and then we meet
at my local pub, McGills.

It has outdated décor,
brown carpets,
mirrored signs
and the signs of ageing,
and good times
are all over the
furniture
and the
frequenters.

They do 35ml measures
and have fitbaw on the telly
and there's always widos
on the jukey
giving it welly
and old Glasgow broads
vape on the sly
and hard-working men
tuck into their steak pies
and we play bridge,
the game his granny taught him
before she joined his papa
in the sky.

We buy
three rounds each
and then we call it a night,
and on the way home

he gets chips
with cheese on the side
and I steal them
and he slings his arm
around my shoulder
as we stride
on the wet chuggy
covered pavement
side by side.

And when we get back
to my flat
we put on
my dad's old vinyl,
merrily sing along
to old songs
and kiss on the sofa.
Wrapped together,
he reads me beat poetry
and with zero authority
we dissect
Motown music
and gangster rap
and I sit
with my head in his lap
and we drink dark rum
until it's time for bed.

I wish it wouldn't end
because by Friday
he's away again,
leaving only
the notes of
his rich
warm
addictive Gucci aftershave
on my pillowcase.

I notice that the cast-offs
from his jeans pocket
have been left on my bedstand,
forgotten and abandoned:
a handful of coins
a packet of Orbit,
and a tiny folded square of paper.

I don't know what I want
it to tell me
because I already know
that I'm second best.
I knew that
he had a wife
when we first met,
and this is selfish to admit,
but that seemed inconsequential,
because me and him,
we felt like old friends,
and it ended up
flirty D&Ms
in the corner of
that mutual pal's thirtieth birthday party,
shouting over the music:
        Two rum and Cokes please!

Then back to so-and-so's
with toe touching toe
on the sofa
under that fluffy throw,
and in the hallway
an unexpected yet
inevitable kiss and
        Shit, is that the time?

There was no chance of a
back-to-mine,
so things were left
rather awkwardly,

parting ways
not really knowing what to say.
See you later,
tonight was mint,
but it didn't mean anything,
even though it did.

Then a couple months later
we were reunited
and I didn't tell him
that I hadn't
stopped thinking about him,
didn't tell him
that I'd been a little bit obsessed,
internet stalking him,
getting jealous,
envious and stressed
when I saw pictures of him
and her,
wishing that it was me.

That we
were a smorgasbord
of social engagements
and spooning in silk PJs,
holidays,
lazy mornings in bed
with Americanos,
the Sunday papers and
homemade granola.
I mean, who the hell
has time for that?

Instead I lied
and acted breezy,
hard to get
but a wee bit easy.
Turns out
poaching a bored

narcissistic married man
is easy peasy.

And before long
it became something:
a little fling,
a Thursday-night thing,
my weekly slice,
euphoric recall.

But it's not enough.
I fantasise about
sharing the boring everyday
moments of life with him;
what I would give
for us to go to the same gym
or watch
as he takes out our bin
or picks up our dog's shit.

I get a small percentage,
a minuscule version
of all that,
because with him
I've willingly signed
a zero-hour contract.

It's now six months on;
exactly twenty-six Thursdays
have been and gone.
I look back at
this teeny bit of paper
in my hands,
a potential portal
to this out-of-reach man.
Maybe
it holds some sort of key.

I unfold it and see
it's just a receipt from Sainsbury's.

CACTUS

The night she told me that she was pregnant
I saw that my cactus had died.
I couldn't even keep it alive.
That made me cry.

NICE GUY

Sorry,
but I have the
best boyfriend
in the world.
I am so lucky.
He leaves me
wee love notes
around our flat,
he runs me vanilla
bubble baths
and I don't need to ask
for him to tickle my back.

I have a sweet tooth,
so whenever he
nips to the shops
he comes back
with a jumbo packet
of liquorice allsorts,
and he treats me
to dinner
more often
than not.

For my birthday
he surprised me
with tickets to *Paree*.
I had a big party
with my whole family
and a bunch of friends
planned,
but, come on,
the most romantic city
in the world.
I knew they would understand.

He's doing a PhD;
he's one of the
smartest people
I know.
Sometimes that can
make me feel
a wee bit stupid,
but it's not his fault
he's intelligent
and so in the know,
you know?

Other women get jealous
when we're out together,
and he can get flirtatious
buying everyone's drinks,
but I don't mind.
I think
they're just loquacious
conversations.
Nothing wrong with
harmless exchanges;
it's a small price to pay
when your partner's so
kind.

We still love getting on it,
having a good time.
He likes a bevvy,
but, I mean, so do I.
I won't lie;
I can get a bit rowdy
after a few glasses
of white wine.

Although sometimes
when we drink
we argue,
but it never gets physical,

just a bit shouty and loud.
He can't help
that he's
stubborn and proud.
We're passionate
in love.
I don't really care
if you don't get it.

We don't bother talking
about the fights
when we wake up;
new day,
fresh start.
Forget about the fiery words
or the comments that hurt,
insults that hit me
straight in the gut.

I'm just grateful
that the heat is off
and we can kiss
and make up.
The making up
is the best part of falling out,
when the dust has settled
and there's no
name-calling
or accusing
or calling me out on
that tiny thing
that I said last week.
I didn't mean it.

He can get a bit nippy,
not controlling exactly;
he has his opinions.

Don't like that makeup on you.
That dress doesn't really suit you.
Be back by eleven.
Kim's a whore, you shouldn't be hanging
around with her any more.
Why the FUCK is that guy looking at you?

What some of my friends call
obsessively possessive
is actually true love.
He's too caring
for his own good.
So what if he doesn't like
other men staring?
Who would?

He's a decent guy,
a nice guy,
alright?
I trust him.
I have the best
boyfriend in the world.
I really do.
I do.

REMOTE

It's Friday night
and we're all alone,
a perfect time to ;-)
but he
keeps checking his phone,
more concerned
with other people's updates
than with his own bird,
his own home.

He looks up.
        Babe, what's up?
I bite my tongue,
preventing all the things
I want to say to him,
my pals' voices
ringing in my head:
        Why d'you even stay wi' him?

We like different pizza,
he likes olives
and I prefer jalapenos,
so we usually go half-and-half;
that's just how it goes.

He'll tan six beers,
then fall asleep
on the couch.
I'll drink more wine
than I should
and watch the candles
burn out.
Squashed together,
legs entwined,
yet we've never felt so far apart.

There we go;
another episode of Narcos
automatically starts.
I put my pizza down.
I'm not hungry any more.
I can't be arsed watching this again;
we've seen this one before.

Long
lusty
weekends
spent in bed
feel so long ago
it's like they happened
to somebody else.

We've been together
since we were fourteen,
so it kind of hurts me
to know
that he'd rather
scroll down a screen
than stroke the place
in between
my thighs,
and our flat
that's too wee for us anyway
gets smaller with every lie.

Lies like *I'm fine,*
I've only had one glass of wine,
I'm too tired,
I left, I wasn't fired,
she's just a friend,
this isn't the end.

But it is.
I'm thinking about

calling time
on this swamp
of stagnant apathy.
How long can you coexist
with someone so unhappily
before you can officially say
we've failed?

Before you admit
it's gone stale
or one of you bails?
We used to be
two peas in a pod,
practically joined at the hip.
Is this just a bump in the road?
A glitch?
A dip?

I was excited to see him
every single day.
Now I look forward
to the nights he chooses to
work late.

I gaze at him desperately
for a sign,
a sign that says
he will always be mine.
He notices me staring,
leans in and smiles
for the millionth time.

> *Babe, can you pass the remote?*
> *The game's on at nine.*

TIARA

I don't like potpourri; it always smells rotten. I loathe that I'm being made to sit in a room full of it. My best friend Lesley is the only reason that I'm not downstairs walking down the aisle right now.

'Make them wait, Chrissy! It's tradition,' she'd practically screeched when I'd suggested I was good to go.

It feels a bit silly, seeing as I'm getting ready in the same building as the ceremony. There's not even a traffic jam we can blame it on. It was Dennis's mum's idea to choose a venue that had everything in one place, including a master suite for them. Of course. From what I have gathered of the planning of the thing, weddings are usually one big expensive culmination of other people's ideas.

I look down at my diamanté Rolex, the gold and silver encrusted face taunting me. Entranced, I sit as the seconds ticker smoothly sweeps around the numbers. I recall the day I received it. One Saturday night last year, Dennis didn't come home after a boys' night out. I did the usual, texted around his best pals, but nobody returned my messages. Sadly, I knew better than to phone the nearest hospital. We'd been here many times before, and it never ended with a police knock and me falling to my knees, weak with shock.

The sound of a set of scrambling keys in the door late on the Sunday night was relief and pain all at once. The thumps of him stumbling up the stairs, tripping over the dog, the double brushing of teeth that almost, but not quite, masked the smell of booze – this was a well-worn routine in our house. When Dennis flopped drunkenly onto the bed, I was turned on my side, facing away from him. No amount of mouthwash can cover up the insidious scent of snorting cocaine in a smoky living room for two days with the same sweaty T-shirt on.

'Baby, are you awake?' he whispered, a hint of fear creeping into his raspy voice.

My body tightened as I ignored him.

It took Dennis under three minutes to fall unconscious; meanwhile I lay awake, my heart stomping in my chest with anger. How dare he do this to me, again and again?

The following morning, he was still passed out, slack-jawed and stewing in toxic sleep sweat, as I got ready for work. I slammed the door as I left the house, hoping it would wake him up in a guilty fright.

When I returned from teaching a classroom of raucous Primary Sevens that afternoon, the Rolex sat, gift-wrapped, on my Egyptian cotton pillow. All was pretty much forgotten. Dennis has blow-outs; that's just the type of person he is, I told myself.

I take a deep breath and look in the mirror, surprised at how much I'm frowning. I pull my 'elevens' – the two little frown lines on my forehead – up and apart with my index fingers like my mum taught me. Frowny lassies get wrinkles, Chrissy.

My reflection looks odd. A petite woman with thick false eyelashes, and slick dark hair scraped back from her face. I feel... daft. I wouldn't be out of place on a competitive ice-skating rink.

I attempt a smile, but it looks what it is: forced. Who am I actually trying to kid? My stomach flips, despite me doing my yoga breathing. I only do yoga because Dennis plays poker on a Wednesday and I don't want him to think he's the only one with a social life. Two can play at that game – oh, yes. He joined a gym, I joined a book club, he started golfing on Sundays, I arranged a lunch with the girls at the same time.

I remember Lesley felt nervous when she was getting married to her man Alex, and, well, look at her now! Three kids and a big house with a two-car garage. Sure, Lesley's self-medicating with a bottle of rosé and a couple diazepam every evening, but perhaps that's what they mean by having it all?

My chest muscles contract and expand in my off-white fitted dress, as if wanting to burst out. I followed the desperately joyless diet my PT Zoe gave me down to the very last stinking smoothie, so I know there's no way I have put on weight. But still, it's uncomfortable. I feel trapped. I look back at the watch, the timely reminder of Dennis's guilty conscience. If this is what cold feet feels like, how could anyone else ever bear it? Unclipping the watch from my wrist, I notice a small uneven patch of accusatory orange fake tan.

'You cannae get married without a spray tan,' Lesley had warned. 'Your skin tone would be the same colour as your dress.'

I suddenly really need a drink.

Just then, there's a knock on the dressing room door. Looking up, I see James, Dennis's younger brother. Physically they look quite similar: they share the same type of goofily handsome face, their bodies are both tall and athletic. Dennis keeps his brown hair short from a visit every fortnight to his barber's, but if he didn't, it would be sure to match the thick and unruly bird's nest that James sports with unabashed pride. James always looks a bit rough round the edges. If Dennis is a freshly pressed shirt, then James is a well-loved wrinkled tee.

A hustler since he sold bespoke porn DVDs to his mates in high school, Dennis is now a remarkably successful cosmetic salesperson, while James is more of a nomad, a true free spirit. One minute he's in China, trekking across the Yunnan province; the next thing we receive a blurry WhatsApp photo of him working at a koala sanctuary in rural Australia. Dennis always teases James, calling him Peter Pan, barely disguising his disdain for his backpacker lifestyle. I secretly think he's doing the opposite of refusing to grow up. At least he doesn't have a gambling problem. Or go on coke benders and turn his phone off for days at a time to avoid his long-term girlfriend.

That's not to say I don't like my life with Dennis. I love it. The gorgeous flat in the West End, the fine dining, the Instagrammable holidays. The long periods of time to myself when he goes on business trips. Or wherever. Yet I've always felt in awe of James's casual globetrotting and relaxed approach to his life. I've been so boring. I went straight from middle-of-the-range school to middle-of-the-range university to... this. Sure, being a teacher, I can travel on my summer holidays, but I cannot imagine Dennis sleeping anywhere other than a five-star hotel. And going solo isn't an option. 'Eat, pray, fuck a smelly white guy with dreads in a bunk bed,' Dennis joked when I casually floated the idea before.

I smile at James. His uncharacteristically freshly cut beard and tartan kilt make me feel so grateful to him for making an effort today. 'What's up?' I ask.

'Dennis sent me to check you hadn't escaped out the window.'

'It's on a latch,' I say back, a little too quickly.

'Are you all set?' James's nose twitches, a small facial tic that I noticed when we first met at a hipster beer hall five years ago. It's a micro-expression that I've always taken to mean he's feeling nerves and affection all at once. I reply by holding up my tiara and flashing my teeth at him. I got them done in Turkey last year; Dennis convinced me. 'You may as well, baby; I'm getting mine done. It's an investment, really.'

Lesley, who is currently hunting down some champagne, left her lilac shawl draped over the back of the gaudy velvet chair beside me. James perches on the chair and takes the tiara from my extended trembling hand.

'I've never put a tiara on anyone before,' James mutters awkwardly.

I shrug. 'Me neither.'

As he leans in to place the ridiculous jewelled crown on my head, I feel his workman's hands brush the tops of my ears. An almost unbearable tingling sensation runs down the sides of my face and along my jaw. I dare to look into his eyes. I notice they are big and brown and shiny, so startling that no metaphor does them justice. As he gently presses down, the tiara's teeth claw at my scalp. I don't flinch.

We sit looking at one another like two deer on a road, vaguely aware in the depths of our unconscious minds that a car could come flying around the corner at any time and kill us both in an instant.

'Where are you off to next?' I finally ask.

'Brazil,' he replies softly.

With horror and exhilaration, I wonder if our faces are getting closer, or is it just that I am noticing him more? A dimple here, a freckle there; he really does have a face that you would never tire of looking at.

Just then Lesley clatters in, a big and busty blonde vixen surrounded by a cloud of Marc Jacobs perfume and cherry vape smoke. She jostles an ice bucket and two champagne flutes onto the dressing table.

'Oi, nae men in here, Jambo – beat it!' she shouts.

James springs up and gestures to Lesley's seat in an over-the-top gentlemanly manner. 'See you on the other side, ladies.' His

130

nose twitch is going at double speed, undermining the smooth charm he is so obviously trying to convey. And then he's gone.

'Bubbles?' Lesley asks, about to strong-arm the cork out of the bottle.

I take one last look in the mirror and say, 'Let's have that to go.'

SMILE

You must behave
but misbehave
when they want you to,
shut up,
don't take up space,
stay in your place,
sit nice,
don't tell tattle tales,
don't show bravery
or be bitchy or bossy
or demonstrate
assertiveness,
don't talk back
or bounce back
or show strength
or resilience,
don't you dare leave,
stay where
they want you to stay.

Always grace your face
with an obedient smile
when a stranger
tells you to in the street,
regardless of the time of day
or if they're in your way
or if you're feeling PMS
or you're stressed
or hurt
or worried
or in a hurry
or grieving
or if you've just had
bad news
or you've been dumped
or you're thinking about

your dissertation
or what to have
for your dinner that night
or a particular situation
that requires you
to concentrate.
No matter how pissed off
or distracted you are, just

Smile!
Smile!
Smile!

Cheer up, love;
it might never happen.
Remember
your gift to the world
is your willingness
to acquiesce;
yes,
good little girls
don't consume
too much alcohol at the pub
or dance provocatively
at a club
and don't ask for it
by not covering up.

In case this message
isn't clear enough:
DON'T
DRESS
LIKE
A
SLUT.

You should carry
a rape alarm
at all times,

cover your drink
to avoid anything
being slipped in it,
walk with your keys
in your knuckles.
Don't talk to strangers
or go home
with people
that you don't know.

Don't
walk
anywhere
alone.

And boys?
You're best to stay within
a rigid cookie-cutter mould.

1 cup greed
2 cups ego (sifted)
1 cup ingrained misogyny (melted)
1 tsp male privilege extract
1 tsp homophobia
A pinch of violent domination
1 egg

Bake in a preheated oven
for centuries
and
voila:
toxic masculinity.

For you boys
the die is cast,
'cause we all know
that nice guys
finish last.
Remember men

have to be tough
and unfeeling
and gruff
and rough
enough to
rough us up,
fuck us up,
treat us mean
to keep us keen.
Big boys don't ever cry;
no, they internalise.

Feed their fragile egos
by putting women down
or try to crush us
with their words
or hurt us
with their force
or talk to us
with their fists
or make weapons
out of their dicks
and we
get screwed
every which way.

In our hearts,
our heads,
in between our legs,
female pain is
inevitable,
ignorable;
his wants and needs
are paramount,
and hers
don't really count.

Our biggest threat isn't
some predator

waiting to pounce
on us in a dark alleyway
but the person
who's in our social circle
or home anyway,
someone we love,
someone we trust.

Those monsters aren't under our beds;
they are in them.

GHOST

I thought we had a good time.
I even gave you head.
Then you decided to ghost me.
Is it 'cause you're dead?

ACKNOWLEDGEMENTS

Huge gratitude to all of my girlfriends, who are an overflowing chalice of wit, stories and support.

Thanks to my Burning Eye Books editor Harriet Evans for her amazing patience and understanding (and for teaching me that fingerblasted is all one word!)

The poems 'Crush' and 'Thursday' were commissioned by the Open Courtauld Hour in association with the V&A Dundee.

The poems 'Chemicals,' 'Nice' Guy' and 'Smile' were all written for the play #GIRLHOOD.

The poem 'Some Girls' was originally commissioned by BBC The Social.

The illustrations and cover of the book were designed by Berlin based designer, the uber talented Robyn Claire Anderson. She brought my ideas to life and added that special something.

Thanks to Miranda Ralston for being so generous and GIFted.

Special thanks to Bryony Robinson, Demi Anter and Eléna de Mello Hogarth who all provided editing support and much needed feedback on my short stories. They helped me tighten up each draft, and are all brilliant writers in their own right.